Celebrating Our Holidays



# Celebrating CHRISTMAS

By Elizabeth Morgan and Arlene Erlbach

Cavendish Square
New York

Published in 2023 by Cavendish Square Publishing, LLC
29 E. 21st Street New York, NY 10010



Website: cavendishsq.com



Portions of this work were originally authored by Arlene Erlbach and published as *Christmas: Celebrating Life, Giving, and Kindness.* All new material this edition authored by Elizabeth Morgan.

All websites were available and accurate when this book was sent to press.

Library of Congress Cataloging-in-Publication Data

Names: Morgan, Elizabeth, author. | Erlbach, Arlene, author.
Title: Celebrating Christmas / Elizabeth Morgan, Arlene Erlbach.
Description: New York : Cavendish Square Publishing, [2023] | Series: Celebrating our holidays | Includes index.
Identifiers: LCCN 2021038574 | ISBN 9781502664747 (library binding) | ISBN 9781502664723 (paperback) | ISBN 9781502664730 (set) | ISBN 9781502664754 (ebook)
Subjects: LCSH: Christmas–Juvenile literature. | Christianity–Juvenile literature.
Classification: LCC GT4985.5 .M67 2023 | DDC 394.2663–dc23
LC record available at https://lccn.loc.gov/2021038574

Editor: Katie Kawa
Copyeditor: Jill Keppeler
Designer: Deanna Paternostro

The photographs in this book are used by permission and through the courtesy of: Cover, p. 1 Goncharenya Tanya/Shutterstock.com; back cover, pp. 5, 7, 9, 11, 15, 17, 19, 21, 23, 24, 28, 29, 30, 31, 32 N.D.Vector/Shutterstock.com; pp. 4, 28 New Africa/Shutterstock.com; p. 6 bbernard/Shutterstock.com; p. 8 Konstantin Tronin/Shutterstock.com; p. 10 MyImages - Micha/Shutterstock.com; p. 13 RoberG/Shutterstock.com; p. 14 Odua Images/Shutterstock.com; p. 16 Suzanne Tucker/Shutterstock.com; p. 17 Eugenia Cherubini/Shutterstock.com; p. 18 realpeople/Shutterstock.com; p. 20 Julia-art/Shutterstock.com; p. 21 RonTech3000/Shutterstock.com; p. 22 DGLimages/Shutterstock.com; p. 25 Angeleyez.of.2/Shutterstock.com; pp. 26–27 Rosamar/Shutterstock.com.



CPSIA compliance information: Batch #CSCSQ23: For further information contact Cavendish Square Publishing LLC, New York, New York, at 1-877-980-4450.

Printed in the United States of America

# CONTENTS

Santa Claus is one of the most famous symbols, or signs, of the Christmas season.

# CHAPTER ONE

## "The Most Wonderful Time of the Year"

One of the most popular songs about the Christmas season tells us, "It's the most wonderful time of the year." For many people, that's the truth. The days, weeks, and even months surrounding Christmas are filled with parties, gifts, and the laughter and love of family and friends. How did these **traditions** start, and what are people really celebrating on December 25? Keep reading to find out!

### The Holiday Season

The time surrounding Christmas is often known as "the holiday season." This shows that Christmas is considered one of the most popular holidays, especially in the United States. Some stores begin decorating for Christmas right after Halloween! However, many Americans wait until after Thanksgiving at the end of November to begin preparing for Christmas.

How do these people prepare? They decorate their homes, bake Christmas cookies, and send Christmas cards to loved ones. They buy gifts for friends and family, and they listen to Christmas music while they wrap them. Even kids can get ready for Christmas by writing letters to Santa Claus,

Decorating a Christmas tree is one way many people around the world prepare for Christmas.

## More Than One Christmas Day?

Most Christians celebrate Christmas on December 25. However, some Christian groups celebrate it in early January, often on or around January 7. Orthodox Christians in Eastern Europe and other parts of the world celebrate Christmas on this later date. The Orthodox branches of Christianity have their own leaders, traditions, and ways of practicing their religion that set them apart from other Christian groups. This includes their January Christmas celebrations.

making Christmas crafts, and practicing for their holiday concerts at school.

### A Special Day for Christians

Everyone who celebrates Christmas honors this special day in their own way. Some people put up their Christmas tree right after Thanksgiving. Others wait until Christmas Eve—December 24. Some people attend church services on Christmas Eve, while others do this on Christmas morning. Others don't go to church at all.

The ways people celebrate Christmas might be different, but the origin, or beginning, of all Christmas celebrations is the same. Christmas is a celebration of the birth of Jesus Christ more than 2,000 years ago. Jesus is at the center of the Christian religion, or belief system, so Christmas is a special day for Christians around the world.

**For many Christians, going to a church service on Christmas Eve or Christmas Day is an important part of celebrating this holiday. During these services, the story of Christmas is read from the Bible—the holy book of the Christian religion.**

# CHAPTER TWO

## THE STORY OF CHRISTMAS

Some parts of the Christmas season are secular, which means they're not connected to any religion. However, Christmas began as a religious holiday, and it continues to be celebrated as one by Christians in the United States and many other countries. It honors the birth of Jesus Christ, who Christians believe is the son of God.

### BORN IN BETHLEHEM

No one knows the exact details of Jesus's life. The stories Christians tell about his birth come from a part of the Bible called the New Testament. According to the Bible, a couple named Mary and Joseph lived in the village of Nazareth. This town is now part of Israel, but at that time, Nazareth was part of the Roman Empire.

The Bible states that an angel told Mary she would have a baby. The baby would be named Jesus, and he would be God's son. Not long before Mary was ready to give birth, she and Joseph needed to travel to Bethlehem to be counted as part of a Roman **census**. They planned to sleep at an inn when they reached Bethlehem, but the inn had no room for them. Instead, the innkeeper allowed them to stay in the stable.

**During the Christmas season, many churches put up nativity scenes, which feature statues or figures of important people in the Christmas story, including Mary, Joseph, and Jesus. People often display nativity scenes in their homes too.**

## When Was Jesus Really Born?

Jesus Christ was a real person who lived thousands of years ago. It's hard to know all the facts about his life because he lived so long ago, but **scholars** have worked for many years to try to find the truth. One thing they're still trying to figure out is when exactly he was born. Some scholars believe he might have actually been born in the spring and not in December.

It was written that Mary gave birth to her baby in the stable. She used a manger—a feedbox for animals—as his bed. Angels told shepherds about the birth of Jesus, and the shepherds came to the stable to see him. Then, they spread the news about the birth of God's son.

A special star also appeared in the sky after Jesus was born. Three magi—also known as wise men or kings—followed the star to Bethlehem and brought gifts for the baby.

## The Life of Jesus Christ

Jesus's birth was just the beginning of his story. When he grew up, he became a preacher. He told people to love one another and that they should be kind. He healed sick people. Many people began to follow Jesus and believed he was the son of God.

Not everyone liked Jesus or believed he was God's son. Jesus was arrested for his teachings. He was then nailed to two pieces of wood that formed a cross, and he stayed there until he died. However, according to the Bible, Jesus rose from the dead and spent time with his followers again. Then, he ascended, or went up, to heaven to be with God.

After Jesus's death, many people followed Christianity, which is the religion based on his teachings. However, many early Christians came from pagan groups, which were groups that often believed in more than one god or goddess. They wanted to follow Jesus's teachings, but they also still held on to some pagan traditions, including their holidays.

## Celebrating the Sun

Christian leaders wanted these new Christians to let go of their old ways. Christmas seems to have replaced **festivals** that pagans held in late December to celebrate the return of the sun.

For people who live in the Northern Hemisphere, or northern half of Earth, winter begins on December 21 or 22. The first day of winter is the shortest day of the year—the winter solstice. This is because this half of Earth is at a point where it is **tilted** farthest away from the sun, so less sunlight reaches Earth.

After the winter solstice, this half of Earth tilts closer to the sun and begins to receive more sunlight. The days become longer. Some people who lived long ago held festivals honoring the gods that they believed controlled the return of the sun.

The Romans held a festival called Saturnalia. It honored Saturn, the god of farming. It ended on December 25 with a holiday known as the "Birthday of the **Unconquered** Sun." During Saturnalia, people held feasts and gave gifts. Northern European people celebrated a similar holiday called Yule. Late December was a time to celebrate!

## Choosing a Date

In the early days of Christianity, the birth of Jesus wasn't celebrated as it is today. It wasn't a major holiday. About 300 years after Jesus's birth, though, Christian leaders in Rome said the date for celebrations of Jesus's birthday should be December 25. That date was already a holiday for

**This shows what a pagan celebration might have looked like in ancient Rome. Because ancient peoples didn't understand science the way we do today, they thought gods controlled the return of the sunlight instead of the changing way Earth tilts throughout the year.**

Romans, so Christian leaders hoped that Romans would stop celebrating that holiday and celebrate Christmas instead.

Gradually, people began celebrating Christmas instead of honoring the return of the sun. However, they celebrated Christmas differently from the way people do now. It was a more serious day. The parts of the holiday we're most familiar with today—the gifts, treats, trees, and big parties—came later.

Opening presents on Christmas Eve or Christmas morning is often a fun family tradition, but it wasn't always a part of Christmas celebrations.

# CHAPTER THREE

## FROM SAINT NICHOLAS TO SANTA CLAUS

Giving gifts was part of the Christmas story in the Bible. The magi brought gifts with them when they visited Jesus. However, the tradition of giving Christmas gifts to other people wasn't part of celebrations of Christmas at first. In fact, it was connected to the pagan holidays Christian leaders wanted Christmas to replace. Even though many aspects, or parts, of those pagan winter holidays changed over time, the tradition of giving gifts remained. Eventually, it was connected to the Christian Saint Nicholas and, later, the popular figure of Santa Claus.

### WHO WAS SAINT NICHOLAS?

In the Roman Catholic Church, which was the first branch of Christianity, a saint is a person honored for their holy life. Saint Nicholas was a Christian **bishop**. After his death in 343 CE, many stories were told about his good deeds, and he was made a saint. Some of the most famous stories about his life were about gifts he gave to people in need, especially young people.

December 6, the date of Saint Nicholas's death, became a holiday in many parts of Europe. Children left their shoes by their fireplaces on the evening of December 5. They believed that Saint Nicholas would visit their house and leave gifts for good

**In some parts of the world, Saint Nicholas Day—also known as the Feast of Saint Nicholas—is still a day for giving gifts.**

children. In the morning, many children found candy and toys in their shoes. This Saint Nicholas Day tradition still exists today.

## New Gift Givers

In the 1500s, a man named Martin Luther started a movement to reform, or change, the Catholic Church. This eventually led to the creation of new branches of Christianity. Many people who followed these new branches didn't like the idea of saints, so they didn't like the idea of Saint Nicholas Day. However, they still wanted to continue the tradition of giving and receiving gifts close to Christmas.

In some countries, new gift givers took the place of Saint Nicholas. In Germany and many other countries, the "Christ child," known as Christkindl, brought gifts to children. In England, children received gifts from Father Christmas, a large man dressed in a red robe lined with fur. French children called him Père Noël, which means "Father Christmas" in French. Saint Nicholas, however, was still the gift giver in the Netherlands. Dutch children called him Sinterklaas.

## A New Name in a New World

Sinterklaas sounds a lot like Santa Claus, and the Santa Claus we know today is connected to this figure. In 1624, Dutch people settled in what's now New York. They brought their Saint Nicholas Day traditions with them. Around 40 years later, the British took over the land from the

# Sharing Traditions

The United States is a nation filled with many different groups of people. Immigrants—people who travel to another country to live there—have come to the United States from many different places. These immigrants bring their culture, or way of life, with them. Holiday traditions are an important part of culture. By sharing these traditions with the people around them, immigrants have helped shape what Christmas looks like in the United States.

Dutch. They also brought their Christmas traditions, including Father Christmas.

Father Christmas brought gifts to British children. Saint Nicholas brought gifts to Dutch children. Eventually, the Dutch and British people in New York began to marry each other, and they shared traditions. Gradually, Sinterklaas and Father Christmas were blended together into one gift giver, Santa Claus. This kind of sharing of Christmas traditions happened all over the North American British colonies, which later became the United States.

**Shown here is an illustration of the French Père Noël.**

**Every family that celebrates Christmas has their own traditions, but some traditions are shared by almost everyone.**

# CHAPTER FOUR

## Where Do Our Traditions Come From?

After the American Revolution (1775–1783), many British traditions, including British Christmas traditions, became less popular in the new United States. It took some time for Americans to create their own ideas about how to celebrate this holiday. Christmas wasn't even made a national holiday in the United States until 1870!

As the years went on, though, certain American Christmas traditions began to take shape. Some began in other countries, and some were entirely new creations.

### Santa Claus Today

When you think of Santa Claus, what do you think of? The image of Santa as a jolly man with white hair, a white beard, and a bright red suit wasn't always what people pictured when they imagined who was giving them gifts on Christmas. A poet named Clement Clarke Moore and an artist named Thomas Nast helped to shape the idea of Santa Claus as we know him today.

While riding home in a sleigh in the winter, Clement Clarke Moore got the idea for a poem about Christmas. He called his poem "A Visit from Saint Nicholas." You may know this poem as "The Night Before Christmas." One of his friends liked the poem and sent a copy of it to a newspaper in Troy, New York.

Close to Christmas Eve in 1823, the newspaper published the poem. Over the next few years, the poem was printed in many

**Clement Clarke Moore described Santa as having a beard "as white as the snow" and a belly "that shook when he laughed, like a bowl full of jelly."**

newspapers. Millions of people were able to read it, which helped the story of Santa Claus spread.

Between 1863 and 1886, Thomas Nast drew pictures of Moore's creation for *Harper's Weekly* magazine. This helped make Santa Claus famous all across the United States.

## Trimming the Tree

Today, Christmas trees can be found in many homes around the world during the holiday season. This tradition has been around for 400 years. The practice of decorating evergreen trees began in Germany around the 1600s. Soon, the tradition spread throughout Europe.

In 1848, an American magazine printed a picture of Queen Victoria, the queen of England, at Christmas. Her family stood around a Christmas tree. Her husband, Prince Albert, was from Germany and had brought his tradition of decorating a Christmas tree with him to England when he married Victoria.

During the 1800s, many German people came to live in the United States, and they kept this tradition. It continued to grow in popularity, and now Christmas trees are seen not only in houses, but also in shopping malls, restaurants, and even the White House—where the president lives!

## Spreading Christmas Cheer

Christmas cards are another holiday tradition that became popular in the 1800s. The idea of sending Christmas cards began in the early 1800s in England. English schoolboys sent out decorated paper greetings, called Christmas pieces, to their parents. These showed how well the boys could write. The boys hoped their good handwriting would earn them many Christmas gifts.

## WHERE DO CHRISTMAS TREES COME FROM?

Today, many Christmas trees are grown on Christmas tree farms. More than 30 million Christmas trees are sold every year in the United States alone. Other families buy an artificial, or fake, Christmas tree. They can keep this kind of tree for many years. Some artificial Christmas trees even come with lights already on the branches.

In the 1840s, the English postal service improved, and it became easier for people to mail cards and letters. One postal service official had a friend named John Callcott Horsely, who published children's books and was also an artist. In 1843, Horsely designed and printed about 1,000 cards with Christmas themes. They sold well, and many companies began printing Christmas cards.

The first Christmas cards sold in the United States came from England. Around 1875, Louis Prang began printing his own Christmas cards in Boston, Massachusetts. Soon, he was selling 1 million cards every year. Other companies copied his cards.

By the turn of the 20th century, Christmas had become a popular and **festive** holiday in the United States. Many of the traditions Americans hold dear today were taking root and would only continue to grow.

**Today, some people include letters in their Christmas cards to tell loved ones what their family has been up to all year.**

**Singing Christmas songs, or carols, is a fun way to celebrate this holiday. Some Christmas songs have a religious meaning, while others are about Santa Claus or other secular things.**

# CHAPTER FIVE

## DIFFERENT WAYS TO CELEBRATE

There's no one right way to celebrate Christmas. Every country and culture has its own traditions. Every family has its own too. It's also important to remember that not everyone celebrates this holiday. Different religious groups celebrate different winter holidays, and some people choose not to celebrate any winter holiday. It's important to respect and be kind to everyone, no matter what holidays they celebrate or how they choose to celebrate them.

### A HOLY DAY

For many people, Christmas is a day to celebrate Jesus Christ. They go to their church for special services, sing religious songs, and pray before eating their Christmas dinner. Christians see Christmas as a very holy day—one of the holiest days of the year. It ends the season of Advent, which is a serious period of time spent preparing to celebrate Jesus's birth, and it begins a season of joy.

## The Advent Season

Many Christians honor the four weeks before Christmas in a special way. This season is known as Advent. One symbol of Advent is an evergreen wreath with four candles standing in it. Three candles are purple, and one is pink. Christians light one candle on each of the four Sundays before Christmas as they wait for the holiday.

Every branch of the Christian religion is different, so their Christmas church services are different too. However, they all celebrate the same thing: the birth of the child they believe is the son of God.

## Other Traditions

Many people who aren't religious still celebrate Christmas in their own ways. They still enjoy the holiday without going to church. They like the feelings of family, kindness, and giving that Christmas is all about. Many modern songs, stories, and movies about Christmas focus on these things rather than on the more religious parts of the holiday.

For example, in 1949, the song "Rudolph the Red-Nosed Reindeer" was recorded. It was based on a book that came out 10 years earlier. The song is about a reindeer that's teased because he has a big, red nose, but then his nose becomes a big help to Santa Claus. It's a popular Christmas song, and today, many children believe that Rudolph is the lead reindeer pulling Santa's sleigh.

**Some people like to make crafts for Christmas.**

There are many other traditions surrounding Christmas that aren't necessarily religious. Some families have gift-wrapping parties, while others decorate cookies or bake gingerbread. Others enjoy caroling for their neighbors. Christmas means different things to different people, and that's part of what makes this holiday so special.

## The True Meaning of Christmas

Christmas can be a busy time of year. People are often rushing around to buy presents, send cards, and bake cookies. However, it's important to remember that Christmas is about more than toys and treats. People in the United States spend a lot of money each year on Christmas gifts, but that's not what the holiday is all about.

The true spirit of Christmas can be found when people stop focusing on presents and look around them. Families get together. People give their time and money to help those in need. Many children and adults sing Christmas carols at hospitals and nursing homes. Sometimes they bring baked goods and gifts.

How can you spread the spirit of Christmas in your community if you celebrate this holiday? You can collect toys to give to other kids or food to give to families who are hungry. You can make Christmas cards for family members you don't see very often. Even the simple act of holding the door open for someone carrying lots of shopping bags or asking a parent if you can help them bake cookies or wrap presents can make someone's day.

At Christmas, many people try to be kinder and more giving toward one another. They think about what their friends and families have

**Many businesses, schools, and communities hold toy drives during the Christmas season for kids whose families can't buy new toys.**

meant to them throughout the year. These acts of love are what Jesus taught about, so it seems fitting that people honor his birth in that same spirit of kindness.

# Make Your Own Christmas Gingerbread

## Ingredients:

½ cup (95 grams) vegetable shortening

½ cup (100 g) white or raw sugar

1 egg

½ cup (120 milliliters) dark molasses

1 ½ cups (180 g) all-purpose flour

¾ teaspoon baking soda

½ teaspoon baking powder

1 teaspoon each: ground cinnamon and ground ginger

½ teaspoon each: ground nutmeg and ground allspice

pinch of salt

½ cup (120 ml) warm water

whipped cream for topping (optional)

**Gingerbread is a tasty Christmas treat! Ask an adult to help you make your own gingerbread using this recipe.**

## Directions:

1. Preheat oven to 350°F (175°C).
2. Grease a loaf pan by rubbing the inside with a stick of butter or spraying it with oil. Then, dust the pan with flour, and shake it until flour has covered every surface of the **interior**.
3. With an electric mixer, beat the shortening and sugar together until it is fluffy and light in color.
4. Add the egg and molasses, and mix thoroughly.
5. **Sift** the flour, spices, salt, baking soda, and baking powder into a separate bowl so no lumps form.
6. Gradually add the dry ingredients into the batter. **Alternate** with the warm water. Mix on medium speed for about one minute once all the ingredients have been added.
7. Bake for 35 to 40 minutes or until a toothpick comes out clean from the center.
8. Top with whipped cream, and serve warm.

# GLOSSARY

**alternate:** To do different things so one follows another in a repeated series.

**bishop:** An official in some Christian churches who is ranked higher than a priest and who is in charge of church matters in a certain area.

**census:** The official process of counting the number of people in an area and collecting information about them.

**festival:** A time or event set aside to celebrate.

**festive:** Cheerful and exciting.

**interior:** An inner part.

**scholar:** A person who has studied a subject for a long time and knows a lot about it.

**sift:** To pass dry ingredients through a kitchen tool that has many small holes to separate smaller particles from larger ones.

**tilt:** To move or shift so as to slant or tip.

**tradition:** A way of thinking, behaving, or doing something that's been used by people in a particular society for a long time.

**unconquered:** Not defeated.

# FIND OUT MORE

## BOOKS

Nelson, Kristen Rajczak. *All About Christmas Carols*. New York, NY: PowerKids Press, 2020.

Owen, Ruth. *Let's Bake Christmas Treats!* New York, NY: Gareth Stevens Publishing, 2018.

Steinberg, Lynnae D. *Christianity*. New York, NY: Britannica Educational Publishing, 2019.

## WEBSITES

**Christmas Around the World**
*www.travelchannel.com/interests/holidays/photos/christmas-around-the-world*
This Travel Channel photo gallery offers viewers a look at Christmas celebrations in a variety of countries.

**"10 Facts About Christmas"**
*www.natgeokids.com/uk/discover/history/general-history/facts-about-christmas/*
This *National Geographic Kids* article features fun facts about Christmas.

**"A Visit from Saint Nicholas"**
*poets.org/poem/visit-st-nicholas*
Visitors to this website will find the text of Clement Clarke Moore's popular Christmas poem.

# INDEX